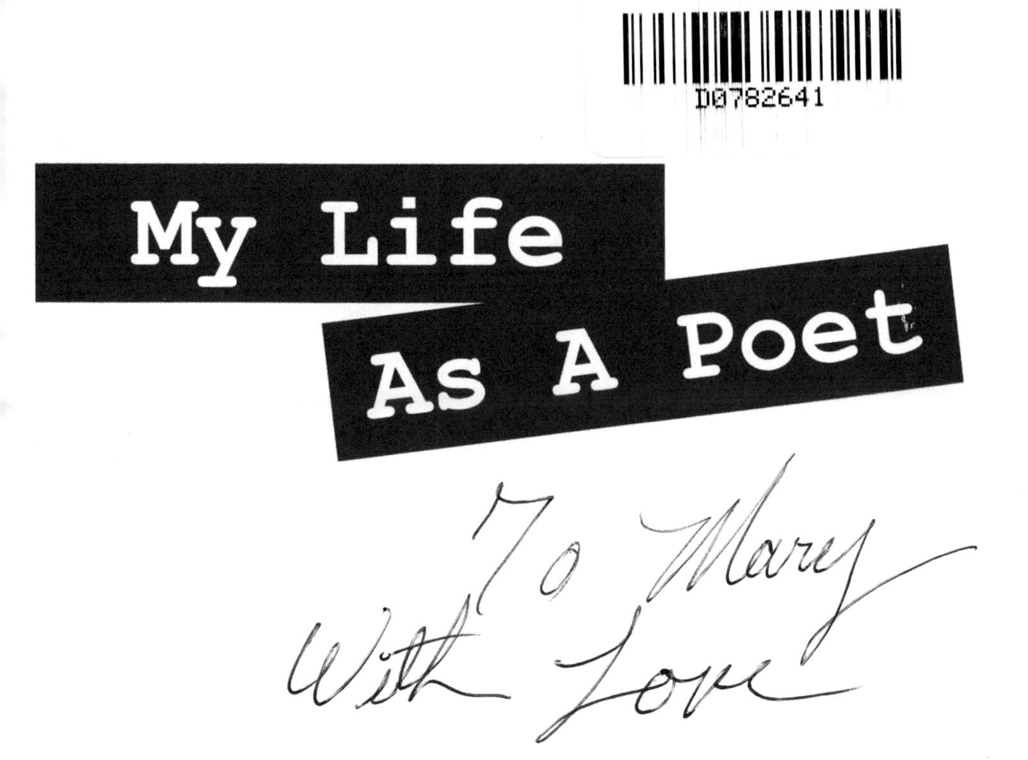

My Life As A Poet

A Journey Of Self-Expression Through Some Of America's Most Turbulent Times

Richard Melvin

outskirtspress
DENVER, COLORADO

The opinions expressed in this manuscript are solely the opinions of the author and do not represent the opinions or thoughts of the publisher. The author has represented and warranted full ownership and/or legal right to publish all the materials in this book.

My Life As A Poet
A Journey Of Self-Expression Through Some Of America's Most Turbulent Times
All Rights Reserved.
Copyright © 2015 Richard Melvin
v3.0

This book may not be reproduced, transmitted, or stored in whole or in part by any means, including graphic, electronic, or mechanical without the express written consent of the publisher except in the case of brief quotations embodied in critical articles and reviews.

Outskirts Press, Inc.
http://www.outskirtspress.com

ISBN: 978-1-4787-4515-0

Outskirts Press and the "OP" logo are trademarks belonging to Outskirts Press, Inc.

PRINTED IN THE UNITED STATES OF AMERICA

This book is dedicated to my mother and father
(Henry & Effie Lu Melvin, deceased) along with my late
brother and sister (Trudy Ross & Sidney Melvin).

Contents

Introduction:

Although I didn't know it, looking back it has become clear to me that "My Life as a Poet" began when I was born; a path had already been laid out for me. I was born 1960 in Harlem, New York City to Henry & Effie Lu Melvin. So began a destiny along with a love of writing that has and continue to shape who I am and what I believe today. When I was about 13 years old, I read two books that made a lasting impression on me and made me want to become a writer. One was called, "Manchild in the Promise Land" written by Claude Brown and the other was, "Down these mean street" by Piri Thomas. The first one was about Harlem and the other was about Spanish Harlem. Both books made a lasting impression which has influenced me as a writer and poet throughout my life.

<u>But what made me want to become a poet?</u>

The answer is simple; as a child I lived across the street from the great African American poet, Langston Hughes. I didn't know it at the time, but for some reason I can honestly say that Langston did stand out to me. I lived in building 21 and he lived in building 20 directly across the street from me. I was intrigued by Langston's ease of living. I would see him at his typewriter all day and night with papers stacked high on his desk. I use to sit in my window and watch him, wondering what he was writing about. What could keep a person typing all day and night? I wondered was there that much to write about? Langston would type and I would watch not knowing what he was writing about or why he did it every single day. Whatever he was doing one thing was clear, he enjoyed doing it. Langston had a calmness and ease about him that I saw in very few people; in fact it's what I remember most about living across the street from this larger than life figure.

By the time I was 10 years old I knew one thing for sure about America. Violence was a way of life here, I saw a President get assassinated, I watched black people being beaten by police all over the south just for wanting their rights. The same rights white people already had. So much was going through my head in those days and my feelings were all over the place. From anger to fear I was well on the road to emotional maturity at a very young age. Growing up as a little boy in Harlem I was surrounded by some very harsh realities and all the turbulence that represented America during that time. I needed an escape and some quiet time. For quite some time television was my place to forget about life. I remember my mother use to say that television was my very first babysitter. Comic books were my next favorite thing and by 12 years old I had become an avid reader of Marvel along with D.C. comics.

As the civil rights movement stormed across the country at full speed ahead; I found myself contemplating my life, thinking about my future, and the future of black people. By then television and comic books had become less of a distraction as I began to become more aware of the realities of racism here in America. Questions started to fill my head, and I wonder where did all this hatred for black people begin? How had we dealt with it up to this point? Where did we get the courage to keep fighting?

More importantly, how was I going to deal with it, and get through it? How was I going to deal with what was going on at this moment in time? My fifth grade teacher, Mrs. Yearby, introduced me to African American history; she began answering all the questions floating around in my head. Mrs. Yearby explained how black people had gotten to where we are today, in spite of the hatred, violence, exploitation, and once being branded slaves. That's when I began to realize how strong and resilient we are as a people. I bring all of this with me into writing and poetry, it's a gift that was given to me that I hope will inspirer all of you. It's my hope that you'll receive every benefit I have from it and more on this journey through this thing we call life.

Richard Melvin, Writer/Poet

Natural Born *Achievers*

From slavery to election of President Obama, Africa Americans are natural born achievers. We had to be in order to overcome impossible odds. It's only when we allow ourselves to wallow in negative emotions and spend all of our energy tearing each other down rather than building each other up that we suffer the most as a people. But when we set a goal or want to realize a dream, we have everything within us to turn it into reality. It's in the very make up of our genes to persist, to endure and to overcome. Today with so many Africa American youth killing each other at record numbers. So many will never even get a chance to evoke a spirit that has served to bring Africa Americans out of the bleakest moments in this country history. But it's not something that just available to Africa Americans but to anybody who willing to let their survival instincts take over when it comes to doing what right for themselves and those they love. As obstacles come up in life that threaten your goals or dreams remember that you're better equip to deal with them than you know, and that we all have the potential to become natural born achievers.

<u>The biggest obstacle we have to overcome, is it ourselves?</u>

There's nothing going on with black people in this country now that hasn't happen to us before,but there is one big difference. The black people of today seem more uninterested, less willing to learn about social change and more hateful toward each other than at any other time in this country history. Self-hate runs rampant in our communities and in our personal relationships. Putting each other down has become a way of life for more than a few of us. But we're scared to death to say anything to someone who doesn't look like us. The problems we have had in the past and how we dealt with them have been wiped totally clean from our memories. Leaving us open to endless debates about what the real problems are and how to deal with them. Disrespecting each other or having some smart remarks for each other is taken as being cool or as coming from someone who really knows what's going on. The lessons left behind by some of our greatest minds, Dr. W.E.B DuBois, Marcus Garvey, Malcolm X, Carter G. Goodson, and Ralph Brunch, Langston Hughes, just to a name a few are not even mention anymore. Our spirituality was a great source of our resolve but now we beat each other over the head with it like a stick. We spew hate about our brothers and sisters from the Caribbean and Africa, we lie about things we don't know about just to make ourselves look good and we never want to take the blame for anything we've done that turn out to be just plain wrong. Like driving up the prices of consumer goods we just can't live without like sneakers and stereo head phones to name a few; with a world of information at our finger tips, some of us still rather talk about what we saw on TV or what we saw in a movie like it reality. Reading meaningful books on our history is almost unheard in so many black communities, unless it's about drug dealers or some big money hookers along with a host of other ghetto stories. Some black women spend hundreds buying fake hair so they can look like someone other than who they really are and some black men will buy a women anything she want to get her in bed before even considering spend a dime on their own children needs. We talk about our youth like we had nothing to do with the way they turned out. It's better to be ruthless than decent, ignorant than educated, selfish than charitable, mean spirited than kind yeah, it all stupid cool! The good news is not all of us are like that. Some of us still believe in our ancestors' hard fought victories and see a way to duplicate those victories today in spite of the odds and confusion. The odds have always be against us here in America, but the truth of the matter is for the first time in this country history one of the biggest obstacle we have to overcome is ourselves.

Harlem on my mind

I remember those cold snowy winter day,
Mount Morris Park is where as a boy I
Played, taking my snow sled down Snake Hill...
It was more than fun...it was a childhood
thrill, 127th Street between 5th and Madison Aves
is where I lived, next to my brownstone
right next door is where I went to my first
School P.S. 24
The end of the school year is what I always
Looked forward too, because summertime in Harlem
there was so much to do, like swimming in the center named
after J.F.K or going to the Loews Theater
near the Apollo to watch movies all
day, If you didn't have any money, you'd stay
on the block we opened the fire hydrant
when it got too hot, So many games we would play...
it's amazing how I could run back in those days
On Saturdays packing bags at the local
A&P was the hustle...but to carry bags home
for someone you had to have muscle
At the night the sound of Motown was all
around...when James Brown came on the
radio…we all wanted to get down!
On Sunday my brother and I were up early to
go to Sunday school being dressed in our
best was the golden rule, after church if you wanted
to go out and play you'd better take off those Sunday school
clothes and put them away
and when the summer came to an end, I
would find myself right back in school
again,

I would think to myself maybe this year
I'll find a girlfriend
Those are the childhood memories I look
back on from time to time
I remember where I came from because
I keep Harlem in my mind

A Recipe for Life

To further the hopes of those
Who have dreams
To give to those who don't
have anything......
To lift the spirits of those who
spirit has fallen down....
To apply the golden rule in
all we do....
And treat everyone in life the
way you want them to treat
you....

Soul of the American Dream

In the American Dream,
We're the church bell that makes freedom ring!
The deep red blood we bled way back in those slave ships
from which they made us come
Is only the beginning of where our claim in America
comes from!
And freedom in the American Dream will never
be forgotten or even grow old
long as America has us as its SOUL!

Do they know about the Harlem Renaissance?

Do they know of the words that came before we started the chronicles of street life, depicting the murders, drugs, guns and how killing off your own kind could make you feel like someone?

Before the cars, gold chains, girls, pass the Moet (champagne) Brother, I'm on my way to jail. Before the violence, profanity and self-hate, isn't that what made most rap music great?

Do they know about the words that came before? The one that establish us to have creative minds you know what racist said we never had and would never find.

When they said we weren't capable of producing literature and art, well the Harlem Renaissance took that theory all apart and open up art's great white door, with the likes of the most talented black writers ever seen before, Langston Hughes, Zora Neale Hurston, Countee Cullen, Paul Robeson, Jean Toomer, Claude McKay just to name a few of those who made it clear that black creative genius was here to stay.

Do they know of the words that came before, do they know the words that gave black men and women across the nation a new face that made equality a destination instead of some unknown place. The ones that made it clear through all the lynching and Jim Crow law that no matter what they were made to do that somehow and some way we were born to make it through.

Do they know of the songs, music, poems, books and plays? That help get us to the equality we enjoy today, however it may go down, in so many heartfelt words is where the spirit of a movement can forever be found. I wonder if they know or is it true, that young black youth don't know or will never care too.

Poetic Soul (A poem for Langston Hughes)

His artistry is for generations of all times, what bittersweet dark chocolate memory do his words bring to mind? Words placed so eloquently on the wind, Langston gave faces to a whole nation of invisible women and men. "Sweet light chocolate prince sing on we'll follow the words long after the music is gone! "Blue, black, white, red, green, his words just like a color scheme, keep evoking vivid imagery of our ever aspiring dreams. So with pen held gently in my hand I pay tribute to this poetic man, His sweet sassy brown chocolate words will never grow old, forever in our hearts a poetic soul.

A Poet's perspective

Like most poets I have a different perspective than most people about the time in which we live. Dante, the great poet had such a perspective of the time he lived in. It caused him to write Dante's Inferno. Poets have always been able to give people a better sense of how they feel and how other feel about the world around them. Our emotion reaction to life and the world around us is what poets attempts to put down on paper, after all feelings or the way we feeling is the bases of a large part of our actions. But it is the poet clarity or unique view of life which satisfy our need for confirmation that keeps us coming back for more. Through words feelings are expressed that we all can connect too, that give us an oneness in the emotional nature of our lives. The times in which a poet lives dictate the subject matter. But feelings are always the same as far as being human goes. Fear, jealous, hate, love, compassion, empathy, sadness, joy, happiness, envy, anger. The poet looks at what emotions drive people to do the things they do. We don't always have to know each other personally to make a connection, just how we feel.

Not Broken Yet

Unlikely to write these words, I
pick up where so many broken
dreams go unheard
I'm meant to be right here until
my end, reminding you as long
as you're not six feet under, you
can still try it again
Whatever it is, if it benefits someone
else as much as it does you, I would
say by all means do what you need
to do,
So as you read and understand these
words, remember dreams are only
broken when they go unheard

Here to Success!

Belief in one self is essential
to success,
The question is…
How many of us are up
to the test,
I say…
It's always best to do all
you can do….
Then leave the rest
to God and pray he
pull you through you!

Message from the Future......

More than a decade into 21st century and our world is changing so rapidly through technology that people can barely keep up with it; as people stay in touch with each other all around the globe more and more. It's has become much easier for an idea or feeling to be relayed quicker and faster than ever before. Pictures, Music, Images, Books, Films, all sent at the push of a button via the web.

But without a vision of yourself where do you fit into this new age? The obstacles we must overcome individually and collective is clearly defined. It the obstacles we either create for ourselves or allow other to create for us that we don't see. The way to go can't always be seen, but we can feel it in each other. Through life, a driving passion or pulse and beat along with a spirit of life or lack of it.

Where there is no vision the people perish, but let us keep that sacred rule. For the rule is golden, treat other as you would have them treat you.

Mind Set

It's not in me to say it can't be done. It's not in me to say we should turn tail and run. It's not in us to sink but swim even if we have to start all over again. Defeat may temperately set us back in task and time, but only success should rules our mind!

Hell's Fires

I'm going to say this once and I hope I never have to say it again it meant for those who don't like us and some of our so called friends
You may take our kindness for weakness that up to you not us, but try and stop us from doing what we're supposed to do and I have no doubt
That you're going to find out what Hell's fires are really all about!

Hearing through Our Hearts

Let's tend to our hearts for one moment through our ears
and feel the next words that we hear
Love, Compassion, Peace
Around the horns of Africa, through Europe from here in the
West, to a war zone in the Middle East
By hearing through our hearts we just may find, a peace we
can all keep!

U.S. Solutions 101

We have more resources than ever before to combat problems that plague us as a people in this country; problems which plagues our working poor along with the middle class. But what right and wrong has been blurred by the elite rich and powerful. They tell us their riches alone can't save our country and that being free to amass millions to add on to the trillions they have, is what has made this country great. But I beg to differ, what has made this country great is the spirit of its people! The spirit of people from all over the world celebrating an idea of freedom put forth by those visionary men so many hundreds of years ago forming this nation we now live in.

The idea that "ALL MEN ARE CREATED EQUAL", I submit it time to reexamine and define who we are as Americans. Time to break the chains of a morally superior image define by an elite class; that wants to sell America out and all of us with it. Until we have shores of Americans being punish for not being part of an economic system design to keep us down and out! JFK warn us about secret societies but they're no longer secret, their operating in plain view. We know who they are; their agenda is clear and so should ours! Take America Back! Our system of government is designed for us to do so! The American system is design for "We the people" to play no small role in how we shapes this great nation and our lives! It's been our ability to pull together under one flag as one people under one idea that has made our country great! As an African American I know only too well the power that has made evil plans for America and also for me and my kind as well. We're on their list as another thing to bring to an end. But it worry me not, for freedom well prevail for my people like it always has here in America and for everyone else if we all stand together!

Bound to grow again

Love like the mind's imagination
is where infinity begins
Even when you feel life has
done you in
Like a tall blade of fresh grass
cut down to it ends
You can be assured love like one
Imagination is bound to grow again

Against the Odd

My spirit ran low where my soul ran deep…
I could feel myself way down where
lowly things creep.
At that point I thought I couldn't make it
and it looked mighty bleak…..
But just look at me now, I'm back on
my feet!

A Prayer for a Sparrow

Trap like a sparrow with a broken
wing, from this heartless cage no
one can hear me sing....
But I'm praying for the day my
heavenly father put a healing
on me and on that day I'll break out of
this lonely cage and fly free!

Inkwell to my Soul

Dipping my pen into the inkwell
of my soul,
On paper I watch all my hopes
and dreams unfold...
With so many lines written from
my heart...
I pray love will keep my people
from falling apart,
And when my time comes to
an end...
I hope they will remember me through
paper and pen

Believe it or not we need all of them .....

Believe it or not we all need those who doubt us, who disappoint us and who betray us. Break our confidences, who offer negative criticism instead of positive criticism. Who basically service no other purpose but to tell us, we can't do it, we're not doing it right, we shouldn't do it this way or that way.
That we're wasting our time and so forth and so on. I'm quite sure you have heard one of tthem before; with such negativities attached to some individuals, you may be asking yourself. Why do I need them? For motivation, to make decisions, to gage your progress, to make you study harder and work longer. To keep you moving and keep you pushing; too eventually prove every single one of them wrong! You may never get rid of all your critics but in the same breathe let me say, don't let your critics get rid of you.

Dear God

Dear God I pray to be always
guided by your hand
Dear God I pray through you
I become a better man....
and when that day comes
when from this earthly
body, I'm finally set free
Dear God I pray there's a
place in your kingdom
for me

Dreaming Again

She comes to me and she's everything
I need her to be
Long walks on the beach holding hands
feeling our toes tingle as we step through
the soft wet sand
In life I'm willing to face whatever will
be as long as I have her right beside
me
She picks my spirit up whenever I'm feeling
down, in her love is where all my joy can be
found
She has made my dream part of her own and
with her I finally have a home
Yes, she everything I need her to be, lover,
Confidant, my best friend....
In her love I'm reborn to a full life where
my soul has no end
then I wake up only to find out
I'm dreaming again

Nothing left to do

I put my faith in my brother man only to have
him beat me down to my knees and hands
I put my faith in my sister woman when I was
Falling apart and she just stomped out
what was left of my heart
Now I guess there nothing left for me to do
but keep my faith in God and pray he pulls
me through
Nothing left to do but pray that the
Almighty pulls me through

From the Ashes

In the ashes many saw what
they thought was our end
But what they really saw was
where our dreams begin
And whoever thinks
Our dreams like ashes can
Be so easily swept away
I pray they bear witness to
our dreams becoming
reality one day!

For freedom cause I was born to fight, from freedom battles
I will not hide, for freedom cause I'll fight until I die....
Richard Melvin, Poet

How I see Black Women

My first perception of black women I have to say came from my mother. My greatest allied and my greatest love; from our gender different my mother set the tone for my love of black women, as my first teacher and greatest friend of my life. Our relationship was strained; but she never wavier in her love, care and support of me. Her love lives on in me today as she wanted it too; she spoke many times of my future without her and my father. When they would be gone and I'd be on my own with nothing but the memories of what they instill in me to live a decency life. So I have felt the protective hands of a black woman's love ever since entering the world. I have lived in their love and lasting affects of it all of my life with much joy along with much appreciation. Black women love has marked my heart for forever.

God's love here on earth,
(A poem for Effie Lu Melvin)

In her love is where we all beginning and her memory
will stay with us until we meet our end
It's her love which has brought us to this day, it's her
love in our hearts that will never fade away
Love given that we never had to ask for, we may find
love like hers before life shut its door but never in this
world we will ever find more
Whether they're here with us or whether they're gone
It's her love for us that will forever live on
A mother's love for us is born even before she has given
us birth and it's the closes thing to God's love here on
Earth

Hard Life for a Black man

Sometime it seem like it all part
of the plan
It's a hard life for a black man...
Brother can you tell me what
I should do?
When it seem like the whole
is against you?
Bite the bullet and do what
you can,
My plan has always been for the Almighty
To see us through cause nothing ever comes easy for me
and you

In the Balance

In the balance is where my life hangs, I can go on to
a brave new world or live more of the same; hated,
disrespected which bring the heartache and pain
Those I thought whose brotherhood was meant to be,
Now sit and plot every means of putting
an end to me,
They take pride in trying to keep my dreams from
getting off the ground, in their hearts is where
the father of all lies can be found.....
In the balance is where my life hangs, but if you
look on God's list for those to be saved from the
Devil's domain, look closely and
you'll see my name!

His Last Words

He brought them love and they gave him suffering
and pain
He brought them God's message and in the end
some loathed his name
Like the thief put to death beside him nothing
less than his death would satisfy them
But right up until the very end to his divine nature
he stayed truth
And some of his last words were
"Forgive them Father, for they know not what they do".

Inner Eye

From the inner eye is where we see what
can't be seen, from there we make reality
out of our dreams.....
The path is not known by any of them who
don't know the road to God's blessing
starts within

In pursue of Happiness

A person has a right to not believe in your goals or dreams you set for yourself, but they don't have the right to take you any less serious or disrespect you because of them. Some people will automatically down play any plans you have for yourself and enlist other to do the same. To form a wall of opinion intended on making you change your mind or abandon any plans you have all together. Should you give into people opinions of who they think you are or what you should be doing with your life? Is there anyone who should have such a strong influence on what you think or what you should do? Taking advice is one thing but do you really believe that listening to other people is the best way to live your life? "It takes half your life before you discover life is a do-it-yourself project"-Napoleon Hill (Author: Think and Grow rich). The plain truth is "If you want anything in your life to come true it's all up to you!" Don't get me wrong in any positive endeavor we're more than likely to gain some support, the question is how much? My experience has been based on my ability to identify who those supporters really are outside of those who aren't truly in our corner; a lot of fakery is out there. But if we're depending on that alone, then we're not giving ourselves the best chance for success is the very lease that can be said about it.

"Spiritual fortitude is always needed in pursuing anything worth accomplishing in life". Richard Melvin, Poet

It is the individual who is not interested in his fellow men and women who has the greatest difficulties in life and provides the greatest injury to other. It is from among such individuals that all human failure springs. Alfred Adler, Psychotherapist

The Philosophy they Live By

Loveless love is all they have to give,
in the seat of arrogance is where they
choose to live
Mocking those who want to help so
many fallen souls their bloods like
the dead of winter runs cold
From the plate of selfishness they sit and
eat their fill, not to mention they'll do anything for a
dollar bill
The down fall of human decency has nothing
to do with them, the philosophy they live
by, only look out for number one

Lennox Lounge in Harlem Live!

"Welcome Ladies and Gents to our Live Jazz
Radio-Broadcast"
"Here from the world famous Lennox Lounge in Harlem. The
black belt of NYC
brought to you by, Reach for your Dream Radio!
"My name is Max Black and I'll be your Host for
this evening, tonight we have the soul stirring
music of Jazz-mania!"
"Performing their new hit "Kaleidoscope" we'll
be going Live until 2am
At which time we'll take you back to the studio
for the debut of our newest DJ Sade Rain"
The Night Bird and believe me she'll do anything
but rain on your parade!"
"The bar is open and at this time we like to thank
our sponsors"
"Coors Light Beer and the distillers of Southern Comfort
for helping to make this broadcast possible"
"We ask that you to drink responsibly and if you don't
have a designated driver
Remember that buzz driving is drunk driving"
"Now it's time for the Gents to spend some money while
the Ladies whip up some honey!"
"I just got a cue that Jazz-mania is ready to go
and now it's time to start the Show!"
And so they go on all through the night

I Count Myself Among Them

Since the creation of paper and pen

Poets have counted themselves among creative men

putting down in melodic terms what it is to

live and learn

The passion, rage, and who's who,

why, truths along with the lies

Sparking the imagination and making dreams

come true, I dare say there's a poet in each one

of you, all down through the ages they have

been among creative men and now I humbly count

myself as one of them

No damn Good (Stories from the Hood)

Whip that booty, that butt, that ass,
time to clip those wings........
Girl don't you know you're too young
to be doing those kind of things
By the time she sixteen she knows
everything
When she gets pregnancy, they say
Girl, tell me it ain't true, cause that
crazy ass boy ain't gonna take care
of that baby or you
Walking with her man that's a boy one
day a bullet meant for him drops her
dead
At the funeral they said
Girl thought she had the one who
would
But one look at that crazy ass boy and
you can tell he's ain't no damn
good!

On the Subject of Love

I'm always touched by my readers who tell me how much they love my "Love Poetry. "Because it brings to mind how many people don't have real loves in their lives, they have people using them at the expense of making them think they care about them or they "LOVE" them. By fulfill that need we all have to be loved, for it was love that brought us into the world or at least the passion of it. So the question becomes? What is true love? Where is it to be found? But the most important question become, when does one knows he or she has it?

Love is like money even if money can't buy love, because you can lose it just as fast as finding it. Which bring me back to my love poetry; love like anything else in our lives is something we all can get better at. The true qualities of love are God like. So if God is not in it neither is love for they are one and the same. Having said that lets look at our own lives; if you never had it, do you know what you're missing? Many people are attracted to someone from the heart and none of us needs anyone to tell us what we feel there. This is what it has come down to in a modern age. To experience real love these days is rare and becoming more rare with each broken heart. Real love is edifying and is evident within its self; enable us to find paths to self-discoveries beyond our imagination; so how does one know when they have real love? By aspiring to be real in loving someone, because we can only get back what we're willing to give. When it comes to love, only in giving do we receive and the love you get back is only as real as the love you give.

Pebble in a pond

I'm a good size pebble
thrown into you a clear
blue pond,
Where the love we share
are like ripples in the
water that go on
and on,
From ripple to ripple show
where our sensual love did
begin,
With us coming totally
together where the ripples
disappear and end.

Each Morning

Each morning I wake up to the
Sun shining in your eyes
The first thing I do is thank God
I'm alive
Then I thank him for blessing
me with you
Because you're the main one his
love for me come through

From Night to Dawn

My eyes sway back and forward
all over the dark beauty that is
you
I know no one else in this world
will do so let's give into loves
hot passions.....
For how every long and we'll
both cherish the memory of
holding each other
Long after the night turns
Into dawn

Beautiful Black Girl

Beautiful black girl speak....
Beautiful black girl sing....
And remember life is never
as bad as it seems
Beautiful black girl give...
Beautiful black girl take...
but try to give more for
Heaven's sake....
Beautiful black girl live...
Beautiful black girl dream...
And the beauty of who you
truly are will always be
seen!

I know it true

In your love I find the strength
to go on
In your love I give you all I
have to give
In your love is where all my
Dreams live
One kiss and I'm reminded
of what I know is true
And I pray every night to the
Heaven above
That I never find out what life
is like without your love

So be it

I love to love you under a clear night
Sky, I love you more as the time
goes by
I want to feel you close to me,
knowing love has a hold on you and
me
No night can sing a sweeter song than
to have it end with you in my arms…
So be it now, so be it then
So be it to the very end

There's no me without you.....

The world seems dreary and the days seem long
without you, hope is lost if not all gone, someone
is missing from my heart and I have no doubt you're
The missing part
My heart is promise to you and only you, so it
has to be clear I love no one as much as I do
you, no passing of time can make my love
for you any less, my love for you only gets
Deeper as time progress
I feel myself fading away my love because
It's true
There's no me without you

The Soul of Beauty

The soul of beauty radiates from your soft
Face with eyes deep dark lovely and
Brown
In your sweet lips the essence of what love
is can be found
Right down to my bone your heart stirring
love touches me
There's no doubt in my mind you're the
soul of beauty

I remember (60's a Life in Review)

The year was 1968; Martin Luther King had just been killed in Memphis, Tennessee. It seemed all of Harlem was enraged and I was 8 at the time. As night came I heard blaring police sirens everywhere. On West 125 street crowds of black people started tearing down metal gates to the front of stores with their bare hands. Theresa Hotel a highrise building at the corner of 125 St. and 7 Ave was on fire. Fires were all the place, FDNY had their hands filled. Meanwhile the police was trying to restore order by clearing the street. But people refuse to move and that when it started, all Hell broke loose. It's to NYPD credit that they didn't use their guns that night, but they did everything else. They began to beat the looters and they didn't care how old or young, male or female, short or tall, fat or skinny it didn't make any different. What I saw that night will stay with me for the rest of my life; it was without a doubt one of the scariest moments of my childhood. I stood and watch as people when hand to hand with the cops. At one point you couldn't tell who was winning. I saw cops beaten just as bad as the people who had been beaten by them. Blood was everywhere. That when I realize at any moment my world could explode with a force I could never imagine.

All can I say is as a Poet that mixing with all colors and classes of people has given me a clearer understanding of the problems facing humanity as a whole. The biggest one being that we're all human and deserve to be treated as such no matter what class, race, sexual preference, religion or gender we are.....Richard Melvin, Poet

Whatever happened to the Black Revolution?

It's a war in our own minds against the
insanity that makes our youth kill off
their own kind
A war against becoming spiritual
depleted maybe a stronger dose
of GOD is needed!
A closer look at what we're really
doing to ourselves that we can't
blame on anyone else.
It's a revolution against who we
are and who we can be
Now is the time to get in touch
And realize the revolution is
inside each one of us

Police Lynching

Modern day lynching that what
I say, when police can kill a young
black man and walk away
In the past so many of us were
hanged from trees,
Now police just shoot us as
they please
Would you believe Cops
have been doing this all
along
I guess no one will believe
that until every young black
man is gone....
The police is where murder
suppose to end
But for young black men in
this country
The police is where murder
begins

When you find yourself among animals, remember people have a tendency to behave the way their treated and now would be a good time to check and see if you have a tail or a heart...Richard Melvin, Poet

A History of killing

Isolated incidents,
that's what the police
say,
While the newspapers
has a story about them
shooting a black youth
every day
They had a weapon,
police saw it hit the
ground,
But for some strange
reason the weapon
never can be found
The same old story
with no end,
Police killing our young
Black men

The war on crime should be against police.....

As far back as I can remember I have read stories of police killing unarmed young black men. That a long time when you consider I was born in 1960 and I've asked myself on a number of occasions when will it stop. But the question I'm asking myself now and that we all need to ask ourselves is why it's still happening after all this time? It seems if we all asked that question maybe we would have an answer by now. But the sad truth is only African-Americans are still asking why? The majority of White Americans have resigned themselves to it being a fact that police will kill black youth based on how they're perceived, as a deadly threat. Whether that threat is real or not doesn't matter, it's what the officer thinks that counts. Being ex- law enforcement myself I would say this would be acceptable if it happen every ten or fifteen years after all no one perfect. But at the rate of two or three killing of black youth nationwide every month is a sure sign that something is terribly wrong with law enforcement throughout this country. Have police nationwide declared war on black youth especially young black males?

It's a crime wave traveling from coast to coast, a murder spree being broadcasted right into our homes! There a new war on crime today that needs to be fought against the police nationwide...Richard Melvin, Poet

Can inspiration be found in a dream?

Keeper of the Flame

In the dark wildness of a dream,
I saw a fire burning in the distance,
too far off to walk it seemed.
But I took one step toward it and
suddenly I was there.
Looking into the eyes of a dark
skin old man with a white beard
and long white hair.
In front of a campfire is where
he sat.
He said, "Sit down my
son and let me fill
you in"
"Before my time in your
dream comes to an end".
Sitting down I did what was only
natural, I said to the old man,
"Who are you"?
He said, "The caretaker of the light
that is inspirational,
which many have used in their lives as
a catalyst for change"

"I 'am the keeper of the flame".
I said, "I don't understand".
He said, "I think you do, you
found the flame didn't you ?"
"I'm here to tell you that the way
You're going in life is right".
"However to make it to the end you
must keep following the light"
"If you don't, you'll go back into the
darkness from which you came"
"Never to become a part of the eternal
flame"
From what he said, I knew somehow
my life was going to change.
So I said, "Old man tell me
more about this flame"
He said, "If you do in life what you are
supposed to"
"You will have overcome great obstacles,
like those before you ".
"The light of your accomplishment will
be added on to the flame".
"So those seeking the light after you can
do the same".
So many questions I wanted to ask, but the
old man seemed to be reading my mind.
When I started to speak, he said, "I can't
answer any more of your questions, I'm
out of time".
Then he said, "I must ask you one
last thing before I leave".
Looking deep into my eyes my eyes
he said, "Do you believe?"

When I said I do, he looked relieved and
said, "Remember my son it is done unto
you as you believe".
He put a small red stone in my hand and
said, "My son whatever you do, keep in
mind what I have told you".
Just then, I woke up and looked in my hand
only to find the small red stone given to
me by the strange old man

All men are created equal

A long time ago when I was a little boy I heard someone say, "All men are created equal" and I knew right then there was something very special about my country. While on a road trip down south in 1966 (I was just six) my Uncle and mother along with me pulled into a place to get something to eat in Virginia. I remember we were going through the front door when a white man met us there to say if we wanted something to eat; we had to go around to the back. I also remember the look on the white man face in back of the restaurant who was cooking hamburgers as he looked at me. I saw nothing but pure hatred in his face, it was a deep seated hate. But instead of being scare those words came back to my head "All men are created equal," I knew right then and there he was wrong to look at me like that. That he had no right to look at me like I was some kind of freak or animal, that even thou I was a little boy, one day I would grow up and be a man just like him, that as far as being a man I would be no more or less than he was. That we were both created equal.

Odyssey

Remembering Yesterday's long
gone sorrows
Marching forward toward tomorrow's
Dreams
We find ourselves forever searching
for what freedom truly mean

Addicted

They want it so much their willing
To fight
They want it so much their willing
To take a life
They want it so much they'll willing to
Throw away love…
They have no reason to believe in
Our almighty up above…
For them darkness will forever replace
Any light
On a path to nowhere driven by their
Need to be right

Soul Man

My destiny was written before I was born,
I was put on earth by God's hands and
by his design I was born a black man, born with a
Burden because of the color of my skin
But because of my soul I was born to win
It's my soul that has gotten me by
It's my soul that has kept me alive
In my soul is where God's love for me
Begins and in God's love is where it will
all end, if I do and if I can, it's all because I was
Born a soul man!

Solitude

In my solitude I spend time with God,
Because he the only thing keeping
My world from falling apart
Living is where all my problems
Beginning
But I know in his hand is where they'll
All end.

The Labor of Love and Pain

Labor of Love
Labor of Pain
Sometime it feels like it's all the same
Some dreams don't come true and
others do
In the end who will make a difference me or you?
Passion is lived out where it
found
Love is what makes the world go
round
The need to survive is what keeping our drive
alive
Labor of love
Labor of pain
Sometime it feels like it's all the same

Longing for Home

Sometime my spirit flies by night in divine
Skies back to the soil of from which I
Came, Africa is my homeland name
The birth place of all humanity and Africa's
Soul will forever reside in me, a life-force
handed down by our creator's hand
I take comfort in the fact we are the original
Woman and Man, so he was with us from our
begin, so shall he be with us in the end
Maybe that when my spirit will go
home again!

Hate is a growing commodity in America.

It's very easy to find hate in America sometime you don't have to look any farer than your next door neighbor. Also it's very easy to find indecency; all you have to do is look at the people we give our public trust to who betray us every day, like police, teachers, doctors also those in city and local government. Corporate America (mainly Banks) goals are to tip the scale in favor of the rich and use average Americans for everything their worth and close their ranks to hiring Americans of color and those on the lower economic scale. What does all this leads too? The decline of decency in America, so when you find yourself among animals, remember people have a tendency to behave the way they are treated and now would be a good time to check and see if you have tail or a heart.

I never knew

I never knew I would feel sorrow so deep down
in my very soul
I never knew my broken heart would only hurt more
as I grow old
I never knew a cold loneliness would accompany me to the end
I never knew I would look at death as my best and last friend

When love gives up

When love gives up on you there's
Nothing else to do
But pack up your heart and
Take what left with you
When love give up on you there's
Nothing else to do
But live in sad memories of
All the dreams that didn't
Come true
When love give up on you there's
Nothing else to do
But sit and wait on love to one
Day remember you

A prayer to be saved

They come to feed on my soul with their lies I'm
Bound, their goal is to drag my life all the way down
It's not the first time they have come to take
Away what I can be, a dream stolen is all they
Have for me; I've been fighting a never ending battle to
set myself free, their evils exist and they laid traps all around
But deep down inside is where my strongest
Allies' can be found
I turn to goodness for goodness sake,
For a spiritual man is one only God makes
Demons without and demons within,
But I know my Saivor will save me In the end

Don't fall

Thank the Almighty
For clarity of heart
And mind
In life confusion is
Something you can
Easily find
But no matter what
Life may bring
If you don't stand
For something
You you'll fall
For anything

Nightmare

What I want to tell you no one else needs
to hear, so come a little closer and let me
Whisper in your ear
That losing your love is the only thing in
This world I fear
Then I wake up and feel you're sensual
Soft body laying right next to me so
Near
That when I realize I was just having
A nightmare

On the other Side of Midnight

On the other side of midnight
is where he take my spirit's
hand
And shows me there's so
much more to being
a man.
A clear full color vision of
what life can be with all
my challenges laid
out before me
A legacy of faith and hope
along with love all comes
from the Almighty up
above, When it comes to
him so many have so much to discuss
But on the other side
of midnight is where he speaks
to all of us

Phoenix Rising

In my loneliness I will not
wither
My bones may bend but
never will they break
I may have nothing because
That something no one
can't fake
But I still rather give than
Take
Some spend their time point
Out the mistakes in me
And I can't help but wonder
If my mistakes are the
Only ones they see
Take your turn putting
Me down
But don't be surprise when
You see I'm still around
Because just when you
Thought it was suppose
To be my end
Just like the Phoenix
I'll rise again!

Risky Business

When love has run its course
and comes to an end
So many of us swear to never
Love again
But loneliness in it's lonely
Solemn bliss
Makes us reason that trying again
is well worth the risk

Shore Bound

Let's keep the hope of love up front in our
Lives for love is never meant to die
Sometime it's lost and it get bury every
Now and then
But love is always meant to be found and
Resurrected again
In the giant sea of love my friend
The waves of love is always
Meant to come in

Spider's Delight

Teeny tiny little creatures that move
In the darkness and have no fright.
Get caught in the spider's web late
At night
And each morning at the dawn's
First light
A hungry spider awakes to his
Morning delight!

Feel New Again.....

Spring brings the roses to bloom, the warm air make lovers
Swoon, birds fly in clear blue skies and love catches every
Lonely person eye, nature is regenerated in a cycle of life to the
Creator end that every living thing should feel new again.

Her love is always with you

For many of us their gone, but the memory
of their love burns on , holding us throughout
lonely nights and all through the storms
of our life; it's her voice telling
us everything will be alright dreams of
time spend with them, is where their love
will never end, because in life whatever
you do, its memories of your mother's
love that will forever stay with you

Torn fabric of Brotherhood

Born of the same mother and father
but now I've lived long enough to
See
A brother not always what he
Suppose to be
Yes, I lived long enough and now
I see that my brother wasn't
always a brother to me
And with so many years passed since
he's seen me, I wonder if he could
Ever be

Black by popular demand

Hard time ahead!
I'm doing all that I
Can,
just doing all that
I can,
Brother don't you know
I'm black because that's who
I' am;
I'm black by popular demand.
I've been told to get a job.
I've been told to get my own
place to stay.
It doesn't matter because I can't
get one without the other anyway.
They don't need me in movies

or T.V., they don't need me on
Broadway,
But Yo! I keep acting away.
"Bruh, why you trying to act like
you don't know who I' am?
Yo! You better pass that
joint like you seen Jesus
my man."
How is it you don't know I'm black
by popular demand?
When he come on the block,
everyone cuts out in a mad
dash.

"Yo! Why folks always know when
I'm going to ask for some
cash?"
The old man said, "Boy anybody
can see you're a poor broke ass."
The sister said, "I'm black baby
and I help out all I can"
The old man said, "With a big old
butt like that; I can see why you're
in demand.
A white boy who's cool with
me walked up on the scene and
said,
"What up my man?"
"I hang out with black by popular demand."
I said, "What up White, you got a
dollar or two."
"Nah black, I was just getting
Ready to ask you"
The old man said, "The government
got it out for you broke-ass white
boys too."
Everybody looking at who's black
and who's white.
But only through the green can you
see the light.
Right now, all I can see is what I can;
I see I'm black by popular demand.
The old man said, "The poor keep
screaming about making everything right."
"But the rich still sleep like rocks at night"

"Hey daddy-O, what up with you?"
Pops said, "I'm on my way out,
how about you?"
"Well old timer, I think I'm
gonna hang for a few."
"Because it's up to me to do
all I can fam, because I'm black
by popular demand."

Staying Alive

When I'm contemplating something beautiful
my thoughts can't help but turn to you
Not only are you gorgeous on the outside you
Have a heartfelt beauty from within
That makes me believe in love again,
some dreams are born to die
But the beauty of your love keeps mines
Alive!

Blue Moon

It's a blue moon rising over me
again, reminding me just how
Hard it is in life to put trials
and strife too an end
Just when you thought you knew,
life has a way of making a
fool out of you
No one has to stand in line
to cry, we'll all get our chance as
Time goes by
Blue moon rising over me again
and it just may be my one and last
Friend

Sixty an Africa American Poet

A Man child born to seek the rhythm and rhyme, as a little muse, Langston's poems played on his mind. the spirit of the sixty's was not for the mild or the meek, on T.V. the nation watched as black folk fought for their civil rights in the street, read a book there, read a book here, if you want to get ahead in life, boy it's reading that will make it all turn out right. Never forget Langton's study of sound, mixing poetry with blues and jazz brother Hughes put it down. Listen closely to the beat of his words; didn't you know soul can be heard? Would a tear fall from anyone eye, if a great Black American art form was to die? I don't think so, but then again, you never know? In the meantime the man child become a man, is that a poetry book I see in his hand? Everyone is free to wave the U.S. flag, I rather stick to my pen and my pad, because there's nothing more American between what's wrong about this country to what's right, than excising our first amendment rights, right?

A Poet's Place

I wouldn't want to trade any
Part of my life
Because my words shine in
God's bright lights!
In the eternal light where we all
can see understand and love that
Meant to be
I'm living through my
Own poetic dream
Where wonderful ideas come into
Reality on faith's strong wings
With no denial in my heart of
God's good grace
In this life all I seek is a poet's
Place

We can sing together, laugh together and cry together but living together is something we all still have to work on….
Richard Melvin, Poet

Building black wealth, it must be done?

The important of developing black business can't be overstated in this day and age; I have mention it on more than one occasion. One of the biggest failures of my generation was to encourage more of our people to explore owning their own business. As it stand now black people spend more money as consumers than any other group in the country, yet black businesses are in a decline and black manufacturers are almost none existent. With the grown of the internet over the last 20 years hundreds if not thousands have started their own businesses, resulting in the creation of more Millionaires than at any other time in this country history. A good job is needed to maintain one self and family but only through business can you build wealth. Now with blacks suffering more than any other group with the recent unemployment crisis; it has become clear that we cannot depend on the job market to meet our economic needs. Is our economic future at a stand still? Yes it is, but it doesn't have to be, now is the time to choose an economic path that will lead to us being able to do more for ourselves and our young people. Building and supporting black businesses is the key to our survival and we have more resources to do so than at any other time in history. To overlook this fact is to condemn ourselves to an economic future in which saying it will be less than bright is a gross understatement.

A Prayer from a Black Poet

What is it that makes us confuse physical love with real love, maybe that why we spend so much time out of touch with our heavenly father above. So many of us chase after the pleasure of the flesh unable to find peace of mind or a path in life that lead to what best.
Overlooking the needs of our young and closing ourselves off from really caring about someone. Focusing on who we can't be or what those who hate us can give instead of living out the life our spiritual father meant for us to live.
Trying to give many what should start with one, so many homes broken up before they've begun. Leaving so many misguided children behind, it's no wonder they haven't got a positive future in mind. Will we be a people who over looked the spiritual nature of who we are over and over again.
Will we be one generation lost from one to another until our very end and fade away? I just know if there any part in this life for me to play it's in point out we're long overdue to start a new day.
A day that's been a long time coming and I may never live to see. When we get back to moral and spiritual values that set us free! When will we get back to truly loving our women and raising our families? When will we get back to taking care of our communities and taking responsibility as a race for getting where we need to be. In our neighborhoods lets finally get rid of the youth violence, drugs and guns.
Let's remembering as a people we either fail or succeed as one. I know you heard it all before but on hope can we really afford to close our future door?
So if there any part in this life for me to play, praying these words will keep us moving on to that new day even if it not until I have long passed away.

Let us pray

Let us pray because we're in so much need
Of God's helping hands
Let us pray because he's the anchor to all of
Our life's plans
Let's pray because our hopes and dreams
All begin with him
Let us pray that he'll see us through once again
Before we bring about our own end

The Dodger

I've dodge the pain of losing love so many times,
I've dodge the self- destructive seeds
By others planted in my mind.
I've dodge the limitations that I have place on myself
I've dodge the longings of wanting to be somebody else.
I've dodge the sigma of my skin color and the feelings
Of being less than
I know no matter how anybody sees me I'm still a MAN.
Ducking and dodging has become a way for me to
Survive
It's how I keep all my hopes and dreams alive!
Ducking and dodging that what I do,
But no matter what,
I just can't seem to dodge the fact that
I'll keep on going until I make it through!

Self-Examination

What the goal? Inform or entertain, to chase after fortune
and fame?
Put my feelings on display or showcase the talent of my
poetic way?
To writing about just myself as if I live in this world all
by myself?
What the goal here? Once in a while I have to ask myself,
Since I'm the only who can
answer that better than anyone else.
I read somewhere words are a powerful thing.
When I think about that I ask myself,
Does it real matter if anybody remembers my name?
If something I've written help brings about in someone life a
positive change?
A change of heart, a change of mind,
To me it's all positive if it benefits humankind,
A little far fetch you say?
There's no fault in you thinking that way,
But remember many a human disaster has been avoided with
what one man had to say, from Gandhi all the way to King.
Check your history books, I'm sure you'll find
a few more either
before, after, or in between, keep in mind,
I'm in no way am' I comparing
myself to the likes of them!
But what if I could play some small part in opening up a few
human hearts?
Now to me that's a something worth reaching for!
It what keeps me writing over and over again!
You can call it motivation, but I call poetry my best friend.

You see purpose is something in life I thought I would never find and just having a chance to accomplish this small goal is fine, because it all I need to leave this world with peace of mind.

Until that Day

From God's love the beast cannot feed it live on our fears sprinkle with greed, kindness to each other is something it can't take it only grows stronger with our hate, but it's not meant for the beast to overtake mankind, for being created in God's image makes us divine, Just remember the battle with the beast will always come again and again as long there's evil among men, but there is a day foretold when the beast last meal will be on those with no soul, And the prince of peace will reign again and the beast along with evil in this world will see its end, So let God's goodness and love be our guide in everything we do and until that day his grace has seen us through

I've seen this Dream before

I go to this locked door in my dream
A door between who I' am and who I'm meant to be
Why do I get the feeling everyone stare at me?
A journey I started in which I find
Love for paper and pen, as I write down my prayers
For this world to come together in the end
In the middle of each night is where I sit
Writing again, as I write in my head I hear myself
Scream, THIS IS WHO I' AM!
Suddenly the door open and I hear a soft
Voice say, Dear Poet come in, as I go through
a brightly lit door is when I realize I've seen
this dream before

Grapes off the Vine

Pluck words like grapes off a vine let the
Taste of the sweet juices run
Through our mind
Savor the natural flavor of what is said
And let their goodness keep
Our souls well fed
If we don't want to eat them, we can let
them sit for a time and those
words like fresh grapes will turn
Into fine wine
Whether we eating or drink our fill
On the vines of our heart grows
What we feel

Posing as a Man

A scarecrow with a hat on
Sit high in a corn field
For a time the crows stay away
Thinking he'll try to harm
Them if he can
Until hunger drives
The birds to figure out
He's just a big old stick
Posing as a Man

Modern Times

We live in the most modern
Of times yet an evil nature still
Plague men minds
Such madness is played out over
And over again
In the hearts of those who didn't
Know when
They had lost their souls before
Ever finding them

Last hope

Let my passion for words consume me
and whatever will be, will be
In looking for my higher self I realize I'm
no more or less than anyone else
But feelings left unsaid will not be where
I finally rest my head
My final resting place will be on all the words
that came from me
And when someone thinks that hope is
all gone
through my words I pray they find the
strength to carry on
Let it be said in being what I was meant
to be, I found what was best in me
For my love of words have served
me well and my last hope will be that they
Serve this world

The Harlem Color Line

At night they came uptown to Harlem to eat some soul food and they came uptown to break all those white rules, listening to that jazz to hear that black song bird sing, they got out there on dance floor showing some bling, all dressed up and doing their thing! The liquor was good and it was a fact no one cared about who was white or black! All through the night that big band did swing and not once did they play the same thing! As day light came the whites got ready to head back downtown, the blacks would say we'll see y'all around and the whites would say don't let this color line thing get you down!

Where the love?

Love of black,
Love of white,
Love of doing wrong,
Love of doing right,
Love of money,
Love of power,
Some people pay for love by the hour.
Love of gain,
Love of pain,
Love of fame,
Love of playing mind games,
Love of a husband
Love of a wife,
Some of us just love to see a good fight.
Love of the left,
Love of the right,
Love of a woman,
Love of a man
In this free market society it's too bad love can't be bought
and sold in a can.
Love of food,
Love of material things,
Love of crime,
On the job some people just
Love to count down the time.
I could go on with love of this and love of that,
but let's separate one fact from poetry, This world won't
make it, without a love for all
Humanity

Praise from a pen

By being a poet I offer the world what's best in me
Words I've written to find a better end
I pray they bring out what's best in men
What we seek is what we shall find
We're long overdue to live through our spiritual mind
In God's grace love can be found
And it's his love I'll praise until that day I forever lay my pen down

Hidden Cure

So many have no feeling for how much better
off their love can be
Their eyes are wide open but
they still failed to see
That lack of love is the sickness and more
love is the only remedy

End of the road for a Poet

Where broken dreams and lost love comes to a lonely end on
the road of despair,
That where you'll find a frail thin poet with pen and paper
just sitting there
He'll tell you how he got there through a series of poems
softly spoken in rhythms and rhymes,
But that's only if you want to listen or if you have the time.
He'll tell you how he was told by so many how they loved him
Only to whine up with loneliness as his closet friend
Then he'll tell you about all his travels and where he's been
along with why he feels
He'll never see those places again
When for this muse you start to feel somewhat sad and dim
with a soulful smile on his face that you would
never expect to see from him,
With soft words he'll say, Please don't feel sorry for me as I
sit here at what may seem to be my end
Because for the love of poetry, I would gladly live the same
life all over again

Odyssey

Remembering Yesterday's long
Gone sorrows
Marching forward toward tomorrow's
Dreams
We find ourselves forever searching
For what our lives truly mean

It never dawned on me beforehand that being a writer/poet would become a way of life which would make me look far beyond the surface of life itself. That it would make me look for the reasons why things are and continue to be today. The why and how or who, which would make a person question everything around them including themselves. "My Life as a Poet" represents the development of me as a person, which I feel would never have taken place, had I not seen that curious man from my window (Langston Hughes) so many years ago in front of that typewriter. It gave me a reason not to throw my life away. It's what made me want to understand people around the world regardless of their color or background. I realized as human beings we all want the same things for ourselves and those we love. That no matter who we are or where we come from, each and every one of us should have the chance to make our dreams come true.

Richard Melvin, Writer/Poet

CPSIA information can be obtained
at www.ICGtesting.com
Printed in the USA
BVHW03s0755121018
529912BV00003B/1028/P

9 781478 745150